WHISPERS

WHISPERS

 **Blair** | HAIKU

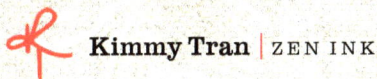 **Kimmy Tran** | ZEN INK

Airen Press
MADISON, WISCONSIN

WITH THANKS TO

KIMMY TRAN | Calligrapher, Chicago
whose Zen Ink renderings give the haiku voice

KAREN BICKERS | Alpha Graphics, Madison
for her steady advice and support

CURT CARPENTER | Designer, Aspen
for his creative energy

KAREN JOHNSON MATHEWS | for being

BLAIR MATHEWS © 2021
All Rights Reserved

ISBN: 978-0-9964454-8-1

 Airen Press

1240 Wellesley Road | Madison, WI 53705
bmathews@wisc.edu

CONTENTS

- 1 **Whisper**
- 3 **Enter**
- 5 **Deep**
- 7 **Glimpse**
- 9 **Patience**
- 11 **Butterfly**
- 13 **Peek**
- 15 **Physician**
- 17 **Night Dancer**
- 19 **Render**
- 21 **Foreshortened**
- 23 **Vortex**
- 25 **Rest**
- 27 **Restive**
- 29 **Vast Silence**
- 31 **Aging**
- 33 **Transition**

Whisper

Meaning's Voice,

Clearer than

Spoken Word,

Listen.

Enter

Breath in,

Enter quiet

Place within,

Breath out,

Reside within.

Deep

Carefully cultivated

Interior viewscape,

The better to see

Other's through.

Glimpse

Eyes burn,

Too many

Untold stories

Seen

Patience

Wind wipes

Recollections,

Weathered memories,

Through time worn

Rock crevices,

Clarity comes

In due time.

Butterfly

Past's lessons

Echo inside cocoon,

Be still,

Listen, inside,

Ask, Grandmother.

Peek

Beauty in shyness,

Cautious smile,

Constrained promise,

Invitation to self,

Others.

Physician

Respect,

Love,

Secured,

Knot by

Knot.

Night Dancer

Grayish white cosmic

Energy waves

Dance outside window,

Heart mind's pillow.

Render

Inside out,

Soul rendering,

Layered brush strokes,

Colored cubes,

Story tellers.

Foreshortened

Quiet fellow,

Passing by,

Passing on,

Before his time.

Vortex

Good friend passes,

Great Grand Daughter born,

Same time,

Same place,

Life's vortex.

Rest

Deep grief,

Love's measure,

Together,

At last.

Restive

Weary late

Afternoon sunbeam

Leaks through

Crack in

Dark cloud,

Ready to

Retire.

Vast Silence

Echoes off,

Red rock spheres,

Thunder Mountain,

Soul's laughter, tears,

Bounce into space,

Other world,

Letting you in.

Aging

Removing

Conditioning's

Cloak,

Child like.

Transition

Sitting still,

Preparing path,

This world,

Other world.

www.ingramcontent.com/pod-product-compliance
Lightning Source LLC
Chambersburg PA
CBHW051604010526
44118CB00023B/2810